To Suture What Frays

To Suture What Frays

Poems by

Jaclyn Piudik

Kelsay Books

Cover photo ©Jaclyn Piudik

ISBN: 13-978-1-947465-26-8

Kelsay Books
Aldrich Press
www.kelsaybooks.com

Acknowledgments

I extend my deepest gratitude to my editor, Nick Kaschuk, whose poetic vision, dedication and faith in my work have made this book possible. I thank my friend and mentor Mark Goldstein, as well as the many other teachers, mentors and colleagues who have offered their insights into and inspiration for some of the poems in this collection, among them, Elaine Equi, Mary Stewart Hammond, Regie Cabico, Hoa Nguyen, Andréa Jarmai, Janet R. Kirchheimer, Barry Wallenstein and Jill Ross. My profound appreciation to Rob Kenter for his time, energy and care in helping to prepare the cover image. I am grateful to Laurie Savlov for his long-time generosity and guidance. And I thank all those who have encouraged my creative, spiritual and academic pursuits over the years. A special thanks to Peter Ykelenstam, for his patience, quiet wisdom, and love.

I gratefully acknowledge the publications and journals in which these poems or versions of them first appeared:

"Banquet of Empty Spaces," "Beckoning Hecate," "De Desiderio Siderum," "The ABC's of Entanglement" and "Why She Ate Her Hair" were originally published in *The Tao of Loathliness, Poems on Cundrie la Surzière,* by fooliar press, 2005.

"Of a More Untoward Obscurity," "Of an Unrequited More," "Of the Nearly Mortal," "Of an Unknowing Verge" and "Of Untenable Prescience" were originally published in *Of Gazelles Unheard,* by Beautiful Outlaw, 2013.

"Questionable Eyes, Brown Hair," *La Presa* 2, May 2017.
"Skeleton Coral," *Three Line Poetry* 42, April 2017.
"The Need to Disappear" and "At the End of Circumference," *Cough* 7, Fall 2015
"Kisielin," *Grandfather, Father and Me,* by Hidden Brook Press, 2013.

"Chanoyu" appeared as "New Year's Eve" in *WV Magazine,* 1999.

"Selections from a Dream Dictionary," *Columbia Poetry Review,* Spring 2000.

"Elsewhere," *Crosscurrents,* Fall 2001.

"The Annals of Red," *The New Quarterly*, Spring 2010.

"Why She Ate Her Hair" also appeared in *Barrow Street*, Summer 2000.

Contents

Bruised Threads

He died on her birthday.
On her birthday?
New Year's Eve.

They sat shiva
on her birthday.
She was fourteen.
        Two times shiva.

Her mother had just made peace with him.
His name was Moe...Morris from Brooklyn.
And the girl?
        Two times shiva.

Winter's feet dragged her
dead uncle through the white

with diamond that cut
mother and brother in two.

        Two times shiva.

The girl born fourteen years early.
The uncle shot for his money
when he closed the paint store

        and the icebank bled.

An omen, they all wondered
that he should pass when she was born.

Mirrors covered in black.
They sat low
in Flatbush that year.

Errata

Dickinson with an "e"

Errata
in this room where five write in pencil
simultaneously scratching graphite, truffles
on pages greedy for space

Errata
A cabbage moth flies out of my purse
transported through the freeze
to late this morning
Thousands of books and I
do not have the heart
to squeeze you out of flutter

Errata
Heaped with rosed salt
catharsis in gouache steps out
of shoes that have been here before

Who said that stars are outdated
that moons are only meant for the past?

Night is relevant still
Answer my call

Vintage Night

Sheep musk and noontime sausage
last for hours
over lightning storms
tinged with ancient Reblochon.
Poppies and potatoes.
Mud and poetry.
No to-go coffee here.

Banquet of Empty Spaces

Black cream, independent of night
Clockwise meanderings at rectangular tables

At first, the need to dazzle   and then to succumb:
the paradox of salt

There is an etiquette to emptiness
an art to voluntary expulsion

a dimension between feeding and being fed
To be dim and vacuous   and then to succumb

Quail eggs teach us the expression of tulle,
the difference between an hourglass and a palindrome

But only you can explain the molecular composition of eros,
why ice floats in water and hunger is thrilling

After the bread   the absence of crumbs   an unleavened ellipsis
No word exists yet for the air that replaces   the need to succumb

Her Greening

North of the well-polished boot,
bodies do not conform
to a French picture.
With heel clicks, the story moves
through the living world gone awry.

Ruin will not await
a tolerance for white bread
or a sudden spell of warmth.

She opts instead for the rustic,
the more important question:
abandoned seed catalogs,
the demotion of vegetable soup.

Garlic, it turns out, is a survivor.
And reality nothing more than a rumor
now, relegated to the archives
after *c* Condiments and *p* Prepared foods, Panaceas.

To have washed dishes here
in this ghost town,
to be blessed with intermittent
goldeneye blooms –
an exemplary bit
of innocence that softens the *l*
of a cardboard soul.

Prickly pear cactus and ripped t-shirts,
the new slogan of the avant garde.
She picks what remain of the *isms*
from among the wild grasses.

And the mountain begins here.

The Need to Disappear

It never really leaves you –
the need to disappear.

On days of wool, it comes like mediocrity.
One arm weak, the other strong.
A moment fatigued
with flexibility
varnished in olive drab.

never   leaves you –
the need to disappear.

I debride the gape of you,
an orphaned panacea,
sure you're not the first.

never   leaves   –
*   need to   .*

He bade me enter
to witness his slow distraction.
We guzzled electricity as if
we were believers.
Now our nightmares come in unison.

–

18

need to disappear.

Jarrings, god-like and underfed,
stacatto patterns flossed with drones,
unsafe emanations.

     never   –
            disappear.

In my dream he said, "I love you, angel."
Morning hesitates, turns to supplication.
Winter in the botany of my eyes.

    It never   leaves   –
    the need   .

A caged desire.
Sewers of faded rain, fat with truth.
The broken lock on a suede valise.
The correct answer.

         leaves   –
               .

A caryatid abandons eloquence
for passing shoulders, soliloquizes
the outline of wind.

never —

You look up and you know that he won't.
Yet he does.
And it haunts you.
But you cannot cry.

Of a More Untoward Obscurity

I will be asleep when the last man answers
a tumult of cemented roses,
when no day equals nine
and we count our reasons for ten more.

Snow pardons the sanguine,
a putrid bouquet pities the weathered.

I won't repent a careless death
or enter the arms of lost messiahs caked in herbs.

The comely moon nestles back to serpentine,
an abridged treble against the elements.

I want sleep to unravel,
unravished for a moment, unsoiled.

Parochial bravos seep in with nowhere to die,
more honest than unstable: an odor malnourished, a noun
mislabeled.

What joyful apocrypha delve into waste.
What joy less somber in semi-clad rhymes.

Cover me from the roar; I come unveiled.
Protect me; all rest unpunished outside my gaze.
Imagine a knowing wades amidst our patience,
words resemble the swell of craving.

I won't be asleep when the last man answers
apprentice echoes limping from the earth.
I will be vibrant; no need for old cures,
a stuttered aquine grazing deep in the 'morrow.

I remember

mothers' meat
snacks and snakes boiling over into skimness.

I remember
gizzards and throat hells
that sent me into tizzy
cobblestone gobbledygook.

Before epistemology
there were carousels and ferris wheels
inane rivers, algae sweats.
Dietary restriction meant no cheesecake.

The popes in Avignon really knew how to live.
Maybe conversion or convergence is the answer
to desire, flagrancy.

I remember lavender fields, squash blossoms
maps of places I'd never visit.
Vagrancy, wanderlust
and 1, 2, 3, 4 years from now
younger than I will be   in…

        decisive, he doesn't remember
how young he will be
ever was or could be.

I remember silver-sparkled platform shoes
pink ribbons, lipstick testers
and Avon ladies

when heart was not a dirty word
or an excuse for a poem
but the edge of adornment

revolved around the geometry
of a soap-stained city.

I remember angora tears and Italian dolls
the essence of fog and smoke
the taste of salted leather.

                    I remember
/soon/
          and bathwater
          when it was
a sweet ellipsis
or someone else's vinegar.

Kisielin

When our speedboat pulled my father
across the surface of the lake on his skis
he carried himself as if this were the life

he truly wanted, as if his voice were
not lost behind the whirring engine
of a 70 horsepower motor in this resort

town overrun now by Hassidim
a reminder of his childhood in Poland.
The ice skates he carved out of pieces

of wood he hid somewhere in the forest
so his father would never know that
he was gliding on ponds, swinging

on trees, falling in creeks, instead of
milking cows, reading Torah,
learning to be a cantor so that

he could cant like his father couldn't.
But he stashed food to eat on Yom Kippur
in those skates tucked under a fallen

tree trunk. Perhaps if he weren't such a rebel
he'd be wearing black robes in Jerusalem,
davening, chanting prayers in his mother tongue.

Under the wig she wore, his mother
seemed to speak to another. She sat
next to the hearth mending worn out socks

with the holes he skated his way through,
saying nothing. She saw the skates on her walks
to the village, heard the shreiks on the swing

as her son flew amidst the branches of
the only wonderland a poor boy could know
in that Eastern European town where

milk doesn't grow on trees.

Pilgrimage

A patch of land
on a road called the end of you,
a cabin of wild peach wood
and terra cotta shadow.

Scarred and smokey, I tiptoe
from chaos to hallucination,
anticipating your veins,
the moony underside of Artemisia.

I crochet the night with skeins
of hand-dyed wool,
elongate the darkness in one steady stitch.

At this wobbly table
waiting in paisley:
the answer to your prayers,
with fiercely buttered cinnamon bread.

Empathic Physics

I used to force you to watch me evaporate,
experience with me the inaccuracy of being.
To sit vigil for my body.

So many moments given up to denying,
to relishing sweet lack.

Desire is obvious, but what tragedy
could take its place?

When hunger is no longer adequate,
language becomes the plainest negation
of ether.

Out of despair, I revert to a Cyrillic alphabet,
to orthodoxy, pantomime.
And imagine that I truly am enviable.

Last year I was the hermit.
This year, a gamble.
Mourning in the company of swords and wands;
the apple waits.
I defrost at 5 a.m.

What would life be without physics?
A lesson in lipstick, inherited bell bottoms?
Treason! Unethical, at the very least.

Two can emulate peace,
but three require compassion
as I saunter   out of quarter-reflection.

Finally—it is the simple gestures
that make everything
stop.

Of an Unrequited More

not to live is to remember
the jealous lull of my pathos

tremble order back to reason
as martyrs dance in a row

delight separates me
a mural demolished, dreams

dye open a fresh delirium
a hearth of yeses

the heart massages
prayer for bone

the night carries
membranes brilliant with venom

old guns waxing
a tulip in the meadow

imprisoned by
the mad regalia of winter

unwieldy melodies dream me
separating the dead

from the nimble cure of silence
what is grist for the body

pores coded with truth
where the wound comes crashing in

prayer to lull
that jealous echo

Beckoning Hecate

But what will happen
when I no longer have slender ankles?
Or when they are not slenderer
than comparable ankles?
Or better still, the slenderest
of all possible ankles?

How will I know myself?

Slender ankles punctuated by feet,
and the toes an ellipsis in third position.

Dance in front of the mirror! he said.
And who is the mirror, I answered
with a question,
already 5/8 sad by this point.
Strangely sour
and self-conscious.

She has power far off, I have heard.
The opposite pole of Dionysus.
Existing in many worlds at once.
Divine guardian of compost.
Yet I want her close on, following
and preceding.

Perhaps then she'll tell me who is in the mirror,
who will be there when the ankles aren't slender.

Revolutions

My trouble is that I am a linen mannequin
wearing blushing workboots,
and these lips are minefields
studded with pomegranate seeds.

I serve grey wine
on the stripe of a flag,
not the checker of a tablecloth.

Days are the typical arches of an eyebrow,
the down arrows at the corners of my mouth.

Who I know is dangerous, vital, paramount,
like rolling back and forth on crushed velvet,
listening to another music,
sipping watered-down garnets
or shots from an aerosol can.

Viva el Amor!

After further reduction
I stoop at his ankle,
curl up in the red
of his yawning breath,
and wait for the end of the world.

In Half

To live life in half
smash the wordless ego
that pines for itself
massacre the minding angel
who hovers at twilight
entre chien et loup

To strive in fidelity
for common things: coffee cups, salt shakers
emasculating rhymes as we go.

Why do you wear your glasses when you sleep?
To see the inside of morning
catch the monarch in your teeth?

There are birds
        and there are words
and there are tongues riveted to confusion

there is trying
        and there is dying
and half of everything is a song without you

you, the lover
the reader, the writer
        who is hybrid
        biblical stallion

Where is the beginning of the wreck
that becomes a thought,
        a wish, windspur, cliché?

Man, I want to dislodge you from question
unsheath my pen from its half-chime:

Philomela get your tongue back
the palimpsested hand
the poem squeezes through

a crack of the lip
soaked in whiskey fiction
cloyed to order.

Chanoyu

She could taste his fingerprints
in the sweet adzuki bean cakes
he fed her on her birthday,
New Year's Eve.
Soba noodles in warm fish stock
from hands that whisked foamy tea in a bowl
300 years older than she was on that day,
and he bowed to her and smiled in Japanese
backing away on tatami mats
brushing his feet on the spotless floor.
The fan he left before her once
laid against the heart under his dark blue kimono.
The only noise in the room
was the flush of her skin as she
drank bitter green liquid jade
that erased all of the broken promises
living in her belly.

Selections from A Dream Dictionary

ALTAR: You are going to die or get married.
Partner is optional.

APPLE, red: You are damaged, but still delicious.

BINOCULARS: In the theatre of the morning,
you are raw with tendency.

GINGER: Dream of ginger's tuberous fingers
and you wish to make love between
the knobby roots of an elm tree.
Your lover will have a bumpy penis.

Alternate: Stay away from cheap Thai food.

HEN, black: You are afraid of death, black eggs,
poached, drizzle twilight on your
forehead. Now go back to sleep, enter
into smooth fields, boots sinking into
mud, sharp spaces in the sky.

LOVER, current: See APPLE, red.

LOVER, former: See APPLE, red.

PILOTING: The Messiah is finally coming.
On a flying crucifix. Send him
to Jerusalem to rescue your mother,
to Brooklyn to kidnap the wife.
Have him leave the horse.
Then, ride bareback to Mexico.

TRAP DOOR: In the terrible honesty of the night
there is safety in the relentless velvet
rubbings of lateness. Despising is mute.

WRINKLES: You have just encountered a sour
angel from another generation.

YARN: Ariadne is in the maze, doesn't want
to be found, doesn't want out, doesn't
want to be found out. She is knitting
wing-shaped sweaters. Clink, clink.
Pearl two.   Shhh....

Notes on Hunger

1.   Suffocating inside stillness
        Listening in time
        to the Middle Ages
        Waiting for something to
        change

2.   You are ravenous
        before our encounter
        I, after – we
        love our wounds so much

3.   There is always something breaking

3.   Coffee turned cold
        smoking, thinking, empty
        ultimatum
        You reached out
        to touch your wife

3.   I wanted the one in the bakery box
        You denied me even that

3.   I find myself craving
        your wrist, the space between
        your jeans and your body

4.   Bite him
        In a room with no one
        Hit him till he loves you

5.   Departing
        You and my abstractions
        One yearning

6.	The evasion of the recognized
	The anxiety of intimacy
	J'aime, Tu aimes, Nous aimons

7.	Amid such famine I live on
	nothing – in perfect
	obedience

Concerto, She Said

a poem in 2 movements

Early in the night's longer stem
what myth bears your sensuous debris?

> *She never asked*
> *to be unglued. Portending tighter places,*
> *she wrapped herself unemphatic.*

If my hair were red and my belly round
might you love me enough
to cry?

> *In the absence of mirrors, no one*
> *spoke ill of her.*

Would you allow me
to devour you?

> *Not all prefixes shun plenty*
> *Nor is every suffix a promise of bliss.*

Or shall I try to negotiate
the waxen riptide?

> *Eventualities issue forth at the midpoint*
> *between fraction and metaphor.*

38

Is it chiseled virtue or something more macabre
that nudges me to cold climates?

> *It wasn't until she saw the sweater*
> *that she knew he had been waiting for her*
> *to die.*

Where can I find the edge
of the storm?

> *On the brink of obeisance,*
> *yield to caution.*

What will I feel if nothing
is forbidden?

> *Such a luxurious now*
> *can only be self-inflicted.*

Slowly in Darkness

The blind one was loveliest.
I was frightened when he uttered fog
that he could see me

that when I open my eyes across his cheek
he would know sunrise

and when I touch him at noon
my hands would smell of fire.

Unrequited Requiem

She was hand,
reading his birthmarks
as if they were braille,
heart *(was it she who invented love?)*
She was hair, haze, hidden,
harlot, hallowed.

{Choir:}   **ILLUMINATA**

Her some-kind-of-blue eyes
stroked, necessarily,
slipping visions
into the folds of him,
concealing translucent verities,
epiphanies, revelations *(hallucinations?)*

{God:}   **FIAT LUX**

She moved slowly through,
groping to reach distant doorknobs,
bannisters ornate with shattered
vitres, refracting toward him
who murmured her glory
at the bottom of luscious stairways
(always moving downward, toward-----)

{Choir, louder:}   **HALLELUH, HALLELUJAH!!!**

Veil crocheted of metallic fibers
remained, strands of radiant
black tears wound round her wrist.
She twisted two fingers at a time.

41

Before the beheading,
he whispered "Bonne nuit."

{Choir:}   **AMEN**

(She was severed in the key of C).

{Silence.}

Of the Nearly Mortal

Today's last arduous grain, an
odeless star – somewhere evening knows.
Today's last hearts dissolve liquid into
icon: conscious among ghosts.

Loss more than leaving; day must go.
The coming into cloud oils impious winds,
bone caves, walled-in pearl towers.
And to die is as much a chore as heredity.

Give to the air a breeze - nothing to the wave.

Take, contrast, delve in
to crumbs of noon
You abhor what is base, pure or real.

Water sobers the mountains,
a valley of few roads
your body shades the violence
of missed hands. One arm where two meet. There
or that. A jail of deaf-dom.

Dogmata

We pleasure in sleep with deluded gods
some gracious cliché hennaed on the soul
wrinkles of folklore and homily, one-
pointed hunger for fugitive poetry.

It eludes me sometimes, the poetry
in salt stains, defiance, even in god-
lessness, pock marks mapping out the odd one
three, five of a face, fingering a solo

in D. These are the howlings of my soul.
A whispered perversion of godiva.
The impossible colors of poetry:
my crinoline - when I choose to wear one –

or a glass slipper that has been unsoled
to hobble awake the real gods and poetry.

Pentimento

A fable is not a fable
when it is locked in a tree

when a goddess lies prone in a car
drunk on martinis

time is an awkward giggle
sepiaed in pork-pie hat
and sulfuric blues

Didn't you know the grail is a stone?
And the mind a spiral?

Turpentine and origin are lacking in the cupboard
and what was once Avalon, is now a barber shop
ensconced in tabs of tie-dye

Pentimento
theatre of temporary doors
the woozy reality that changes
a bloodied tissue into a canvas
a river into a poem

obvious artifice –
why lemonade is square
when you walk through its colour

why the briar in stasis reverts to a swerve
and a voice thrown farther than a whisper
finds resonance in kaleidoscope
wallows itself into the sun.

Blue

You teach me why my innards are stained
glass.

And those things that you hear
Krishna bathing in my blood,
the minor chords between freezing
and burning I – can only wish to.

How can I turn this ladle of rice into sky?
Tell me what I think I don't know of mares and foals,
how we all believe that the world is round
when we hear a raga played on the flute.

Every sun leaves an impression of catastrophe,
and then resumes its original place
in the spectrum. *Lux aetern.* A natural phenomenon.

We observe the coffee losing its translucency
as the cup is filled, collaborate on a requiem
for clarity and the bowlful of berries we just ate.

But theories of transformation have so many variables.
And even darkness gets too crowded sometimes.

Once my pillow was a prism.
I told everyone that it was white
to conceal its true color,
hide the forms that it contained.

Those things that you see –
birds outcircling air,
fertile neon, things Jupiterian,
the boundaries of sound –
the rest of us can only try to.

I know you saw the color of his eyes,
so much like your own,
in that moment of floating,
just before giving in to the shiver
that lies 2 degrees below wisdom, 1 octave below love.
I can only wish I had.

Antoinette in August

Everyone I love sweats profusely
But not her

We suffocate together
smother rants with a plastic bag

She feeds me salmon
to lubricate the fiery air
caponatina and broccoli rabe
crusty bread to soak up
the bitter juices
damp arias and rattled dreams

Once we buried the ashes
of her cat under a tree
where the rain would not go
Once she left to retrieve my soul

She remembers me from the embers
17 stories closer
to Mercury

I put my lips to her eye and swallow
her vision

Smoking moon milk
under an August sky
Sicily far from our
constellation

Someday we will explore
the possibility of lightness

At the End of Circumference

That you are cygneous, arched in disquietude,
unutterably stunning and sparse,
does not assure continuance.

You truss your way through my thighs
with elusions of lingering,
imposing preciousness on paucity,
edges on every viscous mouthful of time.

Fluidity gives meaning to us,
the lachrymose, who subsist on iodized air,
feed on the curves of our own melancholia.

Between the *I* and the *you*
we are nothing
more than the contours of a sob,
an unsynchronized ache,
a subtle lack of lineation.

Cheekbones poised in defiance, we
challenge uncertainty, assume a position
of rondure, settle into a question.

Indigo

Lick indigo ink from my fingers
write on me with your tongue
Tell me it is wine
I will believe you
Tell me it is violet
Tell me it is illusion
and you are a prophet

Tell me it is Roquefort cheese, my prophet
Sapphires chipped away
by Aegean seas.

Deconstructing Buckwheat

Last night she said that poetry is
a waste of paper

and today, I can't find my shell
can't tell the difference between maples

aggregate grievances and ghettos of cool
that wash over me

raw, a myth under my skin
piercing, fiercing eye-dances
hurt me

hurt me, I tell you, and stop…

be as still as those nights
you notice – I
the richer, whistled notes
    the briefer version of female - I

afraid, past present future
the blissful unknowing next

tired of crying and the sweet banjos
that go on for too long

How vulnerable the blueberries can be
though mathematical
    and covert

The luminous edges of Friday
take a u-turn
and the back of you warms to me
distraught and not in Paris

I candy the origins of concrete –
my city of you

Even my wings can't translate the zones
        of shadow
the nowhere more convincing
than compost anchored in light
or the gods responsible for little annoyances.

Asterias Rubens, for the Love of Starfish

The body in the way of itself
tears itself apart

Fingers blue with cold

the poet consoles herself with swank,
vanity, the occasional opera, a clementine.

Yes, she has holes in her stockings
a cosmological hunger

and they said it would be milder today

Scrying for boulevards of grace
forbearance on the real world

she pumps herself for flight like a sphinx moth
losing and gaining altitude
a mania for pirouettes, dangerous maneuvers

You need someone who doesn't feel
so much, so hard, she says

and oh, the miseries and mysteries of plastic wrap!

If it's dark, let it just be night
The bees are gone
and the wheelbarrow mind is enflamed
with forget-me-nots.

She paces the shore of her thoughts
carravaggioed in creamy morning
looking for the red that used to be orange.

Last Will and Testament

after François Villon

Item One:

Wear my eyes when I am gone
that I might know why others stare.
See what is underneath
the marble walkway. Enter
translucency through the gap
between my teeth.

CLAUSE One:
I feel elaborate headdresses calling me,
handsewn truths on luscious fabrics,
brocaded silks in outrageous proportions
creating shapes on my outer ridge.

Item Two:

I leave you, sisters,
crayola fleshtones and blonde hair
(only remotely autobiographical),
Thinness *(always possible)*,
Smiles stored in mason jars
(ready to be decanted).
Freckles in formaldehyde.

Item Three:

My love, I bequeath to you a blueprint
for the architecture of the interior.
Soul and reason conform
to perfect measurement.
Pay close attention to heart size –
Beware improper ratios
and leaky valves.

CLAUSE Two:
There is a struggle between my legs
and sleep, an eclectic array
of warnings scrawled across my hand.
They've already begun to dismember the statues.
And now they're kissing on every channel.
(You know, I was only joking when I said I didn't love you)

Item Four:

I bequeath to you
a falcon from the royal nest,
the deer that bears my name,
the candelabra that once was a tree.
Be sure to wear a glove for protection
from intimate talons and falling pears.

CLAUSE Three:
Lay me on a couch in a city
where the air tingles with butter and cream.
Scatter me along the Corsican coast.
Bury me in a field of fleur de lys,
beneath wild mushrooms on the forest floor.
Give me to sand, seaweed, lilac and lotus.
I am a self-contained diaspora.

Item Five:

I bequeath to you
the song around the corner,
hermetic verses of obscure origin,
anachronistic tenors on viola da gamba,
my voice tattooed with henna and lace.

CLAUSE Four:
Do not contest.
Do not protest your inheritance.
The state of my estate
is not riveted leather
or stoically embossed Victorian walls.
I go farther back, you see,
back to frescoes painted
with elaborate coolness on limestone facades,
back to scarred footsteps,
back to charred velvet.
A train, nineteen inches long,
depthless.

Haiku 1

Amo. Amas. Amat.
How a Latin lover
conjugates.

Haiku 2

A gentle sacrifice.
Broken clavicles have
the power to move a society.

Haiku 3

Solitary leaf
on the subway platform blows
toward me. It knows.

Aftermath of Signs

What power in outer form
You called it a logic frieze –
I, a paucity of dream

The shape of a clump
a brittle grasp of coneflower

Misnomers and miscast almanacs –
why a cup is a cup and not a sweater

If every day had two suns
every hour 102 minutes

I would be older still…

And what is a mythologem, but
the jewel in the poetry stone?

I find my joys in marmalade and chronos
excursions on the way to wholeness

pestered by origins
Platonic colloquies
the habit of ignorance

deliverance in knowing
all beauties have their bounds

in the texture of ether's brocade

eleven syllables
                    enough for a prayer.

Here, in this Nameless Valley

the bedouin women
whine above raw heat,
squeezing pits from olive trees
with their quivering chant.
Tongues, like distant cousins
whirl, ululations
penetrate the veils that hide their faces.

In this nameless valley,
layers of robe embroider
the land touched
by each pair of calloused heels
only once.
Sun filled ewers stand balanced
atop stoic masses of tented fluidity.

Here, in this nameless valley,
under a ceiling of mosaic sky,
hot winds lap sweat
from an undulating torso in squatted trance.
Charcoal eyes roll backwards
as the women dance
to jangling tambourines.

Elsewhere

Still I return to New York...
While in the fortress they roast chestnuts.
Onion tarts melt on red velvet banquettes
and Côtes du Rhône leaks through the ramparts.

Still I come back here...
From prayer-wailing seas where belches are sacred
as olive grease and za'atar and god.
Where words are born in throats deep as wadis,
bundled and sold in burlap sacks next to almonds.

I thought I saw Jordan from my window
when it was merely an urban mirage.
Call my sunflower-visions evasions,
if you will,

but my healer is poetry not prozac
prunes stewed in Armagnac
tulips smeared on convent walls.

I am centuries of cliché in saturnine flesh
an elegy for everywhere
that I am not.

I am the barefoot kneeler in Byzantine mosques
the spinner of soups in cast-iron pots
the creeper through eons
past neons
that singe

the hindsight
the howling
the screeching and scratching
in the cellar
the kitchen
in the attic behind my eyes.

Of Demise and [Dis]enchantment

What remains…Twenty four beauty marks
on my right arm…Two centimeters:
the space between my breasts.

[That part you said you love is still the one I hate most]

The mirror is a cicatrix,
proof that we are
unnecessary repetitions of ourselves,
overfed on disposable moments.

[And yet I could devour you]

Since you dared to make me human
reason is vicious and lazy –
an unforgiving container for tenderness.

What remains…Error denuded.
A small ration of figs.

Rehearsing the ceremonies of the body,
I dissolve into an indecipherable tremor
the queer audacity of softness.

Night

Glutted on white sleep,
I lick the lips of flowers,
contemplate how to travel
up a furrowed brow.

Seven roses later,
thorns don't hurt.

Solace comes, if only momentarily,
in cataract darkness,
the muffle of unspoken water.

With hoarse step,
we penetrate each other's dreams.
Squatters,
vandal angels graffitiing the walls
of some uninhabited heaven.

In your midst, I am pure
                              coincidence.

In your midst, hell is
                      a kinder hunger.

Oh, to lie with the wind
wander with you from swell to swell
inhale your tears &
bathe in fire.

De Desiderio Siderum

Virgin, I belong to no man,
but to the anarchic society of plan[e]ts,
to the heedless, seeking nothing
more than hunger itself.

Mere embellishment
the moniker he bestowed upon me

I am maddened animal vegetable mineral, spitting
precious gemstones
onto armor and headboard in intricate patterns.
I am loyal servant, bearing the stone of exile.
Yet hag, beast, ensorceller, other.

It was an angel who taught me
about stars. Sky C follows Mandala A.
Mandala B is beside the sacramental black.

And now I can tell him everything
he wishes to hear.
That I love him, that I hate him
that the planets portend nothing favorable,
only kingship or leprosy,
that rocks do not emit stereoscopic messages.

That there is grave danger in beauty:
worst of all, not being taken
seriously.

Charred by the sun,
discontented but never uninspired,
as dusky insouciance,
I am condemned for wanting
more than the luminous body.

Solitude drips
long hair into a stream.
People with bowed heads – everywhere.

Everywhere –
shades of probability
repeat themselves.

Pink

The legend of a minor cupcake. Why rain
is wetter than snow. An animated panther.
Looking askance, pimples and nipples. Hand-tinted Marxism,
photoshopped souls. Equity and certain cheeks. Quartz.
Tallchief's toes, Phoebe's nose, fairy tales, dildos.
Phalluses and fallacies, thwarted indecencies.
An anorexic tongue before the blade. Comatose
bubble gum. Orthodox linen. A viral eye. The guru's scent.
Lapses, tristesse, highlighter, my lips. Floyd's wall,
Victoria's secret, sun stains. Manicures, watermelon meat,
rare fish, a sow's teat. Radioactive ice cream,
retrograde tears, the extra stripe in a sock. Discombobulated
gravity. "Thank you for shopping here."

An impermanence of roses under the skin.

The Annals of Red

Crimson. Where do sins go?
Scarlet? Which memories become poetry?
Polysyllabic blushings over form.
An allergic reaction taken for rubies.
Force feedings. A lackluster suicide.
The arm of Eve. A Rubens study.
What shame is there in desiring to know?
Voluntary anger. Having perused.
To strand, to pierce, to kiss.
To incarnidine.
Periodic cessations result in a loss of bone density.
A rose by any other name—
is probably not a rose at all.
Love. Hate. Rage. Communism. Acne.
Mistakes. Edits. Magenta. Mars.
Auburn tresses. Hope in accordance with fire.
The way out of Oz. The way out of Egypt.
The Vikings. The Sioux. The Confederates.
Scabs. Wounds. Sirens.
She learned to stave off the wolves
with a basketful of strawberries. Rubicund.
Florid. Flush. Ruddy. Sanguine.
Ritualistic scarification. Ripening.
A used tampon. Clairol hair dye nos. 256 and 278.
A cardinal. A robin's breast. Macoun, fuji, jonagold.
Cedar. Some ants. Ladybugs. Sunday brunches.
The reason they invented Visine. Barbarism.
War paint. Tilakas and bindis. Henna tattoos.
Magic markers. Crayola crayons. Childbirth.
Gashes. Galoshes. Grottos. Darkrooms.
Danger. Stop. No Entry!
Couldn't they see she had been crying?
Valentines. Sunburn. Fall. Frostbite.
Cabernet. Pinot noir. Ketchup.
Campbell's soup. Chili peppers.
An Arizona desertscape.

Terra cotta. Teakwood. Clay. Brick.
Copper. Vermillion. Ballet slippers.
Persian carpets. Kali. Santa. Rudolph's nose.
Inflammation. Irritation. Oxidation. Coke cans.
Kidneys. Cells. Unhealthy gums. Lipstick.
Nail polish. Rouge. Hibiscus. Sumac. Roots.
Pompeiian temples. Brothels. High Priestesses.
Satan. Joker. Doctor. Butcher. Painter.

And when she died, they punctured her wrist to find color.

Canción of Rust with Warm Milk

Try to convey a lullaby.
The joy is all – a square of love
renamed: an ankh, a needle –
no guide.

To ponder grand envy can be mortal.

To mire in you,
to prey on magic –
last of all nevers.

I make the black seem washed,
undermine breath as faith's confusion.
I tempt you to seal the dew,
forsake the tides, find pleasure
in a cruel eye.

I beg for collapse, a dirge
sewn under the skin,
the debt for living
treeless and wild.

In precious death I respond
to your need for exile.

The dawn bursts in
drunk on rusted ink.

The rite relents.

Vicissitudes

Dreams yoke themselves
to delicate nerve endings
to fragmentary realities.
A moribund partnership
of calamity and goat.

Folded in a white dungeon
eyes stray, talk of meaning
voice mired in a catalogue
of timbres.

Night is easy to do.
The blank of a forearrm
horizon of a knee
four naked membranes
and a grapefruit's carcass.

To maneuver   refrain
reminisce   require

light matches
dark

complected
        circumstances hang
numinous
in the grotto

temptation
beneath the cleft
of the smallest
                        arch.

Instructions for a tranquil existence:

Keep dragonflies at bay
Maintain obsolete forms of a sliver
Forecast closure

Of an Unknowing Verge

Soul lamented: pour me
amber bread in evening,
diffused with Corona and verbena.

Grainy days will be a moor
nowed in the soon-to-be's.

Lacking company, unwashed of evening
de-scar me, jarred in map and genus.

Coarse days will bring
sandpapered roses, vanilla on velvet.

Soul unmended: pour me
the countryside of leaving

abrade this body into being
unknowing who I will be.

Life

I've been to hell and enjoyed it,
to Florida and didn't.
I've eaten enough Brussels sprouts
to become an honorary citizen of Belgium.

I can speak Parisian French,
unorthodox Hebrew and dream
a dawn song in northern rhyme.

I have starved and vomited,
swallowed and spit.
My mouth has been a gateway to love.

I've been with Aboriginal wannabes,
Biblical wives, Mexican waifs
and polygamous matchsticks.

I used to smile more,
wore velvet hot pants and platform shoes
between Torah and Talmud.

I've been a green witch and a good witch,
live for rituals and visuals,
vertiginous papers awaiting fruition –
to grow into disenchantment.

I take comfort in convents,
and dowse my way out
of the forest when lost.

I've drunk Japanese teachers
with flecks of gold and opiates,
been a victim of metamorphosis
by the peer of medieval blue eyes.

I am what remains
after an elaborate experiment
in alchemy.

Miles from Raw Cotton

There is something soothing
in a mouthful of marrow and regret,
in the sweet profanity
of how you must taste now.

Here in half-naked fictions,
ideologies poole candlewax
onto a thick mahogany table.

Between the promise of fury
and what is forgotten, always
this desire for coarse landscape,
a longing for stringy curtains,

that want induced so easily
at dusk, coaxed without effort
from its resting place,
under a twist-off bottlecap
or in a bed of random cracks.

The ABC's of Entanglement

For you I'd gladly give an inch of ash,
I'd gladly be your Botticelli baby
and welcome you into uncertain curls.
But there is danger in disheveledness,
it threatens equilibrium,
entanglement will surely make you fall.
I can't explain the genesis
of my demented hair
nor can I tell you why it is
that I still speak some Aramaic jargon.
You've tried to brush through all the kinks,
to decipher my untraceable lingo,
but knots there are too many
and language comes from nowhere,
no etymology, no origin.
You fear this head without a part,
your balance is in question
from wisps and words left rootless –
literally stranded.
You are disturbed by these tresses
that despite all attempts remain unkempt.
My dear, you thought I had no venom.
Ah, but you were wrong;
Medusa doesn't live in Xanadu.
She knew she couldn't count on combs
and you would never lead her into Zion.

Lune Quintet I

Skeleton coral
A finger painting stuck to the sky
Some autumns are combustible

**

An anorexic fire
craves oxygen to fill a
smoldering hollow ember

**

Choreographed edges blur
Freedom of movement blends us
into one continuous limb

**

There is nothing
but above and below
and how you divide them

**

I want to be
the short end
of your wishbone

Sanctuary

Could I expect you to stay
inside unyielding walls

where beauty is pure illusion
and each week we reconstruct
our edifice, this gothic dollhouse –

where equilibrium exists
despite fragility?

We breathe through porous stone
protected by our sacrilege

and forgiveness finds us, seeping
past immalleable granite

never ungiving, a structure
softened, quietly running

through extended fingers
that cannot take hold.

Questionable Eyes, Brown Hair

for Marguerite Duras

What is heroic in watching a fly perish?
Who is responsible for that raspy voice,
the horn-rimmed glasses, the rice paddies?

The body evacuates itself when necessary.

I'd take her admission of promiscuity as invitation,
but I am wed to a chain of eccentricities.

Her city has entered my adrenals,
giving off time-released doses of resistance
and the sweetest architecture,
the familiar monotones of the Rue Oberkampf.

The greatest icons are the bashful ones,
the brooders, immortal
but never free from the burden of aging.

What is heroic is how long it takes to die.
Oh, if I could squeeze into that body
when this and all others fail me.

A Prayer for Insomnia

The awful beauty of our collapse—
what justifies the right to be desirous,
startling an almost dormant need for disarray.

Nothing disrupts the moment of craving.

Roused by a feared delight,
threat of incandescence or an otherwise disgraceful seduction,

the subdued evolves into exquisite anarchy.
Numbness awakens into echolalia.

Unwitting, we conspire with the moon to reinvent ourselves
and mundanity is rendered obsolete, resistance surmountable.

The most elegant unrest is the one we never choose,
imbibed with disbelief and breathtaking.

Lune Quintet II

The bow peers
longingly at the cello
he will never stroke.

**

Orpheus' abandoned lute
plays on without
missing you.

**

Totem and mannequin
desirous, do not
overcome immobility.

**

We are two continents about to
embrace despite our chasm.

**

Modigliani face grows
on trees. Washed out Pagliacci
in laughless bonnet.

**

Of Untenable Prescience

To yoke the water for no reason
to be a wind-cadenced syllable.

Without eyes, the night abandons me

its teeth shine with heat
as yellows inundate rest.

How brilliantly loss dents a heart
and the little bitternesses invade evening

having lunched on roses at midday.

I resist sunset, defer to venom
as black cacti open to the rush.

Allow me a handful of planets,
teach me the knot of your throat.

I tried to compose a history of spring

                                      Late spring
Tar scented afterbirth

And you impatiently waiting for leaves
                     to identify themselves

Self Portrait, In Ordinary

Tracing stains along the sidewalk
their bloodshot eyes erase me

as I forage for a voice and wade
through endless *why do you look so sad*s

I wish that someone would write my biography
that I would know how to live
the rest of my life—

      is this the sign of a messianic appetite…

My tears are no wetter than yours, it's true
no more saline than a statue's

and crying, I have learned, is as useless
as trying to climb trees felled in a storm

      tears only make for mascara streaks and swollen lids

but to translate me
without them would be a deception.

In dark dimple

        we collaborate on a kiss.
Cheekbones parenthesized by half moons:
scars from the forceps.

Cartography

{Mapping the Colors of the Soul}

Envy me this languid malaise, this precious
epithet, still trembling in its octarine.
Thick with infinity, it allows but few
heart-things to enter.

Breathing has escaped me. For now I rummage
through unconsciousness, inure myself to
its euphoria. I am unworthy of
this violet sleep.

In the glyph between my eyes, where once you lay
serpentine, you revealed the perimeters
of chaos, a world complete but not wholly
taintless or unbruised.

Be my psychopomp. Take me to places
older than the kingdom of the tongue, that I
might fathom the ineffable, deconstruct
the name of silence.

My core is venous, watery musculature,
where prelapserian visions seep from
verdigrised valves and tears are sequestered, left,
for a brumous iris.

You are sulphur, alfalfa-sweet, tempered with salt
and mercury, bearing me secret messages.
I pretend you are air, metal, citrine, the
warmth in my belly.

Fire in the palm of my hand, the nexus that
binds a hubristic sun to earth. We expel
ourselves into random ascents and falls, submit
to apocryphal splendor.

Parsing bodies, willing ourselves prosaic,
we recover physicality, paper
and blood, evolve into the reddened rings
of the alder tree.

Devil's Alba

after John Milton

Lost among the barking orchids,
what is beauty becomes as
violent as the spread of leaving.

The hour approaches when owl-light dims
and eyes narrow, when tobacco blossoms
close and hoard their covert perfumes,
when even the Great Unholy fears
the profanity of dissolution.

And Satan sings:

You, the only-adored of all,
are the forbidden names of God,
the talisman of naive mariolaters,
who do not know your bellow,
a prayer of blasphemy at eventide.

You are the fleshly idol who steals
the end of identity from archangels,
the verge of timelessness, a copse
swallowing Vespers and Compline
and Matins into your dusky shelter.

This stricken seraph is pure
obeisance before you, kneeling
at your ebullient altar, coming
from realms shamed into glacial plateaus.

We grasp at shreiking shadows
as they withdraw into mornfall,

when we will be wrenched from
the harborage of our tenebrous oubliette,
uncoupled by the drear of dawn.

Immoblized and fallible, hovering
above gateways and gravel pits,
while illumination flirts with pangs of gloaming
dejected wings vanish into daylight.

You Brand Me with Memories of the Morvan

The lightning, turbulent
over the Burgundian mountain.
Thick-skinned provincials
who cooked up a storm
for my skinny, skinny body.

Then I needed to be empty
to feel electric.
Then there were no words,
there was no darkened
skim of you.

What matters
is lightning,
currents streaked
across a charred sky
leaving a hint, a silhouette
of mountain ranges,
old trains that take hours
to get you there

to the place where hunger
is sated by lightning storms
crackling like the voices
over the hearth. Like bones.

Still I long for lightning storms
and a skinny body.
Now I have yours
to create a spark
that combusts
like a pear dripping
with cognac.

You brand me with memories of the Morvan
where wild boars remain exotic
and God is still a burning bush.

Tripta

Some sonnets resolve themselves,
immune to mood swoops
convulsions grammatical, libations parodic.
We love our monkey gods
thoughts pollinated by jade and hay.
Sliced jugular,
martini for a ramshackled soul.

Barefoot and bleached, no token to Oz
the hollow of a raspberry is sweeter when it rains
a prayer is always electric.
We trip over memories of our name.
Without locusts or hugs
saturation comes in 37 years
resolution in 14 lines.

Morph-
Ologies

I anthropologize
to all those wondrous kooks
who kiss on escalators

the handholders who
secret themselves in broken glass
giving distance to light

Air touches air, surd
electrified by its own science

ever lost, ever culled
tripping restless into fire porches
ice, eternity

I am thinking of what it must feel like to
                    melt
a skyful redaction of daze
a two-fisted tree
in a hemisphere
outside the poem
outside the mindfield
outside the gaseous mementos
          of a word that never happened

I am thinking of fahrenheit
bricks exploding from their rinds
sequences of extinction
a mosquito unfeeding itself
transfusing my skin
from its other language into wax—

under the rain it is frank and fearless
challenges the equator
to break like a bar of soap
to breed a new moon-place

where the eye suckles a growl
and there is no end to raw.

Why She Ate Her Hair

Because she lived in the house of hunger
                              emaciation nation
                    the state of starvation

Because she ran out of sky
              and this could bring heaven

Because she needed definition
                         to be angular

Because if she ate enough of herself
                    she might find herself

Because mortality was not enough
              and surely god was hairless

Because they accused her of being
                    full of herself
and she thought she'd prove them right.

Notes

These poems were written between 1998 and 2015, mainly in New York City and Toronto.

"Kisielin" is for my father, Isaac. Kisielin is the name of a town in Poland (now the Ukraine).

"Chanoyu" is the traditional tea ceremony in Japan and is for my teacher, Kimura Sensei.

"Concerto, She Said" is from the Latin, *concerto, concertare*—exert, to exert.

"Blue" was written for my friend Arnaud in memory of our beloved Frédréric.

"Last Will and Testament" is after *Le Grand Testament* of 15th century French poet François Villon.

"De Desiderio Siderum" is Latin for "on the desire for stars."

"Questionable Eyes, Brown Hair" is for the novelist, playwright, essayist and filmmaker, Marguerite Duras, who wrote about her childhood in French Indochina.

"Cartography {*Mapping the Colors of the Soul*}" was written for a collaborative project with composer Toby Twining. The piece was performed as part of the Non Sequitur Festival, curated by the Composer's Collaborative, at New York City's Lincoln Center in August 2001.

"Devil's Alba" was inspired by John Milton's *Paradise Lost* and the figure of Satan. An *alba* (or dawn song) is a Medieval courtly love lyric which originated with the troubadour poets of Provence. It is a poem in which the clandestine lovers express their dread of the approaching dawn and thus, their inevitable separation.

'Tripta' is dedicated to the memory of Marisa.

"Why She Ate Her Hair" was inspired by a 19th century photograph of a young anorexic woman who died from ingesting her own hair. (*Van Dyke Print, "Stomach Encased in Hair," 19th century.*)

About the Author

Jaclyn Piudik has authored two chapbooks, *Of Gazelles Unheard* (Beautiful Outlaw, 2013) and *The Tao of Loathliness* (fooliar press, 2005/2008). Her poems have appeared in numerous anthologies and journals, including *Contemporary Verse 2, The New Quarterly, Columbia Poetry Review, La Presa* and *New American Writing*. She has edited three collections of poetry for award winning Canadian publisher BookThug and is the recipient of a New York Times Fellowship for Creative Writing, and the Alice M. Sellers Award from the Academy of American Poets. Jaclyn holds an M.A. in Creative Writing from the City College of New York and a Ph.D. in Medieval Studies from the University of Toronto.

Kelsay Books

www.ingramcontent.com/pod-product-compliance
Lightning Source LLC
Chambersburg PA
CBHW071101090426
42737CB00013B/2424